AF407940

Mama, I Met A New Friend at the Diner Today. He Said He Would Be My Forever Friend!!

By

Sandy Black

515 South Flower Street, 18th and 19th Floors,

Los Angeles, California, 90071

ISBN: 978-1-83663-003-6

Library of Congress Number: 2022915634

You may visit her at her website: booksbysandyllc.com
and email: blackbrunson5@gmail.com

This book is a work of fiction. Names, characters, places are a product of the authors imagination.

Table of Contents

Dedication:

To the 'loves of my life', and the memories we shared.

Acknowledgement:

To All my high school classmates and family, who contributed to this book. Although names have been changed, you may just recognize a few.

Chapter One
But I Don't Have Ten Cents.
That's Okay, I Got Enough!

It was a warm Saturday afternoon. Preacher Black's wife looked out the kitchen window where she had just put three freshly baked pies on the window sill to cool and said, "Bruno, you and 'Kitty Manxy' go down to the Dandy Diner with Blacki and Andy Brins for a soda. She's the little girl you met coming out of church Sunday. She just came from California and hasn't met any friends yet. You help look out for her, please." Blacki's mother had earlier, after Sunday morning church, asked Miss Brins if Andy liked ice cream cause Blacki's Uncle Harlo owned the Dandy Diner. He always gives Bruno, the big, ole yellow dog with a droopy, dripping mouth and a growth on his ear and his constant 'cat with no tail' companion, scoops of ice cream. They serve as self-appointed bodyguards for the family. Looks alone deterred any bad-acting characters that might be up to no good.

This was the first time Andy had been to a real soda fountain Diner. The Greyhound bus they took from California only stopped at bus stops, and it was reported to best not eat the food - you might just die. Miss Brin had several friends who fixed little sacks of sandwiches, fruit and homemade cookies. Little candy, individually wrapped, was slipped inside. Andy did not stop talking about the

Diner, which had a soda fountain in it, for days on end, especially when she talked to God in her nightly prayers. Thanking him for sending a new friend. Sort of like KC.

The next Sunday, Andy skipped down the church steps because there was to be a church picnic afterwards, and it sure seemed whenever there was a picnic after church, the preacher had to pray for the entire congregation, and she was hungry. Bruno and 'Kitty Manxy' were waiting outside. Andy giggled, "They sure are a funny looking pair!"

Blacki said, "They look even funnier when 'Kitty Manxys' feet get hot on the pavement, and she rides on his back." Andy remarked, "Oh well, people always say things about me being short, skinny and have loads of reddish, curly hair like an Irish lass." Blacki laughed out loud.

Blacki's father and mother were the new Pastors of the little, white, cottage-style church on South Cherry Street. Bruno told 'Kitty Manxy' that Blacki was rarely out of the penalty box because what he didn't think up on his own, the self-appointed Village took delight in monitoring the mischievous, busy little boy. Bruno declared, "Why that old bag that dresses like she comes from or going to a funeral every day, told Blacki's mother that she saw him, 'Kitty Manxy,' and me taking two chicken legs from the church pitch-in table BEFORE the Pastor had prayed for them." Why, that ain't true", said 'Kitty Manxy'. It was Charlie Ruggles, and it wasn't two. It was three." Bruno said, "The chicken was sure good, but the punishment wasn't so great."

That little tattletale event postponed the four newfound friends' next week's planned trip to Dandy Diner for an ice cream soda. However, the next Saturday, Uncle Harlo told Blacki if he swept off the sidewalks and Andy wiped off the ten bright red stools along the counter, they could choose any flavor of ice cream. This was so great because each flavor except vanilla cost 3 cents more a scoop. And Uncle Harlo kind of knew they didn't really have ten cents, and they had been falsely accused of eating 'unprayed for' chicken.

Dandy Diner looked fondly at the two cute little people who were working to earn their afternoon sodas. Blacki got done first and went in to help finish wiping off the stools. Sooner done, sooner sodas. Dandy Diner remarked how that little, onery scamp seemed to be quieter, more well-mannered and polite when with Andy. "Maybe his parents should get him a little sister to watch over," laughed 'Kitty Manxy.'

Dandy Diner grinned, "He would make a cute big brother, wouldn't he."

Days and weeks went by. Blacki, Andy, Bruno and 'Kitty Manxy' went to church on Sunday and most Saturdays and could be seen walking to the Dandy Diner throughout the summer months. Bruno carried his buddy on his back, and as escorts, they enjoyed a nice, cold ice cream reward.

Andy announced in early fall she would be moving to the farm with her grandparents, and her mother would no longer play the church piano nor would she get to go to the Dandy Diner. The day they were to leave, Andy's Grandad, she called him, stopped near the courthouse fountain so Blacki, Bruno and 'Kitty Manxy' could say goodbye. Andy had become so fond of her friends that it was hard to leave, but going to her grandparents to live was a dream come true.

As the car left, Blacki yelled, "Bye Andy, maybe next summer you can come to town and we could meet." Andy waved, hung out the window and said, "At the Dandy Diner, okay?"

"Oh, I forgot something. I didn't spend my ten cents. I'll save it for next time."

Bruno and 'Kitty Manxy' were seen grinning at each other. Blacki looked sad. He hoped he would see his friend again someday.

Chapter Two
The Whistle Diner With A Secret

'Kitty Ahhgee', considered to be the Whistle Diner heroine, is a favorite around the root cellar, which she guards jealously. She often exhausts herself 'being in charge.' Since the railroad accident and the loss of her arm, 'Kitty Ahhgee' moves gracefully through her perceived ownership of 'her' Whistle Diner. Her green eyes snap everyone into service.

The Whistle Diner, named after the #10 Train that has continued to run through town, blowing its whistle like a well-wound clock signaling the time of day, is a reminder that preparation for a new Diner season has begun. It was expected that families who passed through the Diner would be treated like Royalty, and the long-time staff would continue to be dedicated to excellence, pay attention to detail and help make The Whistle Diner a 'destination'.

The Whistle Diner smiled, watching 'Kitty Ahhgee', as usual, taking her job very seriously. It was Tuesday. Peach Cobbler Day. 'Kitty Ahhgee' ran ahead to make sure the very best peaches, ripened just right, were put in the small basket for the cobbler. The beautiful peaches were neatly stacked in wooden baskets in a secret place. Outside the Whistle Diner, a rock wall lined a path to a long-kept secret. A root cellar built underground covered by brush. 'Rooty' yelled at 'Kitty Ahhgee', "Come on in, long time -no see!" "I know, laughed 'Kitty Ahhgee'. It seems as though our winter season ran on and on." "Up here in these mountains, one never knows. Some days, it was hard for anyone to get down my narrow path to visit, remarked 'Rooty', but the peaches are just as though we plucked them off the tree yesterday. I can smell the cobbler all ready. Guests always ask. 'Where did you get those fresh peaches?' Another Whistle Diner secret!"

"Well, we open this week. Let the games begin! 'Rooty,' did you hear any scuttlebutt about needing extra revenue and maybe sprucing up the Root Cellar to hold tours inside? They would add a little extra on meal costs and rename it **The Whistle Diner and Root Cellar."** 'Kitty Ahhgee' grinned and said, "So, it looks like you might see more of me over the next six months if that happens." "Wow, that's awesome. Look forward to it. It does get lonesome hidden down here sometimes."

Doors opened for the season, and activity is at an all-time high. Being the only Diner in a one-hundred-mile radius, everybody shows up hungry.

'Kitty Ahhgee' looked up from her soft round pillow near the front door and yelled, "Good glory! What on earth! Is it a bus, a van, a moving house?" The door opened, and four adults, eight scraggly-looking children of all sizes and ages, two dogs, and one tiger-looking cat poured out into The Whistle Diner parking lot. Clearly down on their luck, It looked like smoke was coming out from beneath the hood. 'Kitty Ahhgee' whispered to the Diner, "It's warm enough we can feed them in the outdoor garden, but I'm not sure that rattletrap they came in is hardly fit for the road."

The biggest cat 'Kitty Ahhgee' had ever seen hobbled across the lot. A beautiful, orange-striped cat with three black paws. He stopped, and his large hazel-colored eyes focused on the most beautiful creature he had ever laid his eyes on and two gorgeous green eyes glaring at him.

"Hi, pretty lady. Are you from these parts? I'm 'Kitty Tige! I am with the Toyer caravan going to Logan, Utah. We are dairy farmers, but we have been 'called' to go and help assemble and play the new Tabernacle pipe organ. We hope to settle outside Logan, raise sheep and dairy cattle, make quilts and just follow our traditional ways. Our bus of orphan children will live away from the abuse they have endured and among warm and friendly people who will do them no harm. I lost my paw in a hunter's trap, so I am in charge of watching over the little fellas who are too young to work. I no longer can help with the cattle and sheep. Honestly, I love this job the best anyway."

'Kitty Ahhgee', already mesmerized by this new visitor to the Diner, was speechless. "I'm 'Kitty Ahhgee', and I live and work here at The Whistle Diner. I, too, was orphaned some years ago, and The Whistle Diner owners took me in after the train accident." "Sounds as though we both are blessed to have had people who cared for us." smiled 'Kitty Tige.'

The Logan, Utah travelers were sidelined for two weeks due to the huge Northern Arizona rains and the possible danger to their precious cargo. Turns out, the radiator was the culprit, and the caravan stragglers had an opportunity to catch up with the disabled van.

In the meantime, The Whistle Diner and its guests were treated to singing and playing on a miniature piano by Mrs. Toyer. She had insisted at the beginning of their journey that her hand-made walnut piano made by her grandfather would go with them if nothing else did. The children played hide and seek all around 'Rooty' under the watchful eyes of 'Kitty Tige' and 'Kitty Ahhgee.' They were so well behaved, quietly saying their prayer lessons and other schooling with few primers. Piano lessons were a daily exercise as well. Everyone laughed at the little musicians who played more off-key than on.

The Whistle Diner and the locals collected clean and gently used clothes for the caravan children. Each of them was front and center, shining like a new penny for church the Sunday before departing for their new, permanent home in Logan, Utah.

The two cats had been inseparable and clearly were looking at each other and asking, "What are we going to do? Logan is many miles from here. We might not see each other again." 'Kitty Tige' said, "I don't know how or when, but you WILL see me again." He leaned up against her armless shoulder and whispered, "I promise."

The Whistle Diner and the popular root cellar tours became a destination for settlers moving west for a new life.

A few years later

'Kitty Tige' was seen sitting outside watching a little one-room schoolhouse. He patiently waited for the door to open and the piano to stop playing, signaling it was the end of the school day. The school teacher stepped out, and eleven children came running out. Behind them was 'Kitty Ahhgee' followed by two of the cutest tiger black striped kittens.

The Whistle Diner had earlier reported some settlers going to Logan, Utah, had an extra 'stow-a-way' passenger.

'Rooty' waived goodbye and vowed not to snitch until the caravan was halfway to Logan.

Chapter Three
Two Sister - One Allowance

Myrt and her younger sister, Sady, each got an allowance for certain around-the-house chores. One problem. Chores had certain standards, and if followed incorrectly by house management, the allowance was reduced even to nothing at times. Example: Whoever was to dry the dishes had to make sure the washer of those dishes left no food on them. That alone cost the dryer one half allowance. Dusting without picking up the assorted knick-knacks was another. Myrt declared there were 150 ric racks sitting everywhere. Who looks for dust anyway? Many years later, her housekeeping reflected her dislike for dusting.

Sady looked at her sister, who was taller, bigger and a year older with hair to her ankles and said, "I want to go to the Lutz Corner Grocery and get us two boxes of butterscotch pudding. Their five cents will buy us the two boxes. We can go home and cook one, and there will be another for Friday." "Come on, Sady, you know Vernon told me he was going to come to the Rexal Soda Fountain Diner as soon as he got off work, and he will pay for our sodas."

Sady frowned at Myrt and grumbled, "You know we are going to get in a heap of trouble. The whole Whit family attends our little country church. Mother said last week, " The Whit boy, who insisted on sitting by Myrt in Sunday church, is too old for her. You are not to hang around with him. Understand?" Myrt quickly told Sady, "We are not hangin' out with him. For cripes sake, we are having a phosphate soda, and if he pays, we will save our allowance money to buy your butterscotch pudding."

'Kitty Ebony', the coal black, only female of the litter, trotted along with the two sisters, who had decided to go for the phosphate sodas. She climbed up on her usual spot on an old milk box and looked forward to getting a little cup of cool milk in her small cardboard container. The little companion seemed to have a sense when the two teenage girls might not use good judgment in their decisions, such as meeting a boy at the Rexal Soda Fountain Diner in broad daylight.

Vernon arrived, and he sort of looked like Elvis, or at least Myrt thought so. His blonde hair was slicked down on the sides, and his tee shirt was rolled up at the arms where he had a pack of Lucky Strikes rolled up in one of them. 'Kitty Ebony' said, "We are dead." Vernon had a new car and always seemed good at making suggestions as though they were the right thing to do. He paid for the marshmallow phosphate sodas and then asked the girls to take a spin through the nearby park. "Sady reminded Myrt that they had Church Youth Fellowship at 5:00. "No problem," said Vernon. Myrt sat in the front, and Sady and 'Kitty Ebony' were directed to the back seat. 'Kitty Ebony' said, " At least none of those nosy church ladies will see us here in the back." Usually, Myrt and Sady would walk to Woolworths or Lutz Corner Grocery and dream about how far their next allowance might go. Afterwards, there was just enough time to get to Church Youth Fellowship. At 6:00, they would walk home. Today, the 'spin with Vernon to Mounds Park twenty miles away, not Whitestone Park around the corner' got the girls back at six. Vernon dropped the girls off at the corner, and they walked home just as usual.

"Nobody's gonna know we weren't at Youth Fellowship. Mother has been sick with that eye infection and hasn't been to church in two weeks." Sady, who was too scared to ever tell a lie, could not figure out how to tell her sister what corporate punishment looked like. Myrt had been raised by an elderly California couple and adopted, while Sady was taken to Indiana by an Aunt and raised under the house rule "Children should be seen, not heard," and a few other rules and regulations. Sady figured Myrt might best learn them a little at a time. When the old couple passed, Myrt was put on a Greyhound bus to go 'live with her sister'. Sady was of the mind that God saw everything and was watching. 'Kitty Ebony' said when they were dropped off, "This ain't gonna turn out good".

A couple of days later

"Someone answer the door. Reverend Harge is here. Let him in." Shortly after the Reverend had inquired about the progress of their mother's eye and prayed for its healing, he said, " I'm so sorry you girls missed Youth Fellowship on Tuesday. I thought you might be bringing Vernon Whit with you. He sure has a nice car. I hope he uses it in God's work. Reverend then said his usual visitation prayer and left, telling the girls he hoped to see them next week. By that time, Myrt and Sady were calculating how many years they were going to be in solitary confinement. Especially since Myrt was already planning her next Vernon excursion.

'Kitty Ebony' went to the Rexal Diner the next day and reported that the sisters were not dead or anything. They were wishing a month of "YOU CAN DO NOTHING' house arrest would go by fast, but each day seemed longer than the day before, especially since the chore list was one hundred times bigger. At least, that was Myrts' assessment. NO ALLOWANCE, of course. They were allowed to go to Sunday church but had to sit on each side of their mother. Vernon mouthed 'I'm sorry' to Myrt. She grinned. Sady tried to plead her case, saying she was an innocent bystander. She lost her appeal.

Two Years Later

Vernon and Myrt exchanged vows on a warm, June day right after high school graduation. Sister Sady was Maid of Honor, and Reverend Harge presided.

We are told all five of their children were in attendance at the 25th Anniversary celebration. Vernon still had his 1952 Chevrolet, which usually sat in the garage, but today, he and Myrt had shined her up and were going to the Memorial Day parade. They waived at the Rexal Soda Fountain Diner on the way by. Myrt said, "Do you think they still make Marshmallow Phosphate Sodas?"

Vernon grinned.

Chapter Four
Mama, Please Let Us Go to the Diner!
The Jukeboxes are Coming Today.

"Diane, Betty, Nila, Deloris and Emma are going to get there early and save seats at the counter", Laura told 'Kitty Pearl', who was standing at the door waiting on approval so they could bolt down to the Daisy Diner. Laura had planfully done all her chores, including some on the list for later in the week. She had even taken all the doilies, soaked them in buttermilk, boiled sugar water, and carefully dipped them. All were drying upside down on big glasses. That seemed like a good insurance policy for getting to go to Daisys Diner.

The six teenage girls had pooled their money so Mr Jacobson, owner of Daisy Diner, would not have a reason to make them leave because they were taking up space from paying customers. He called it 'boy lookin.'

It's 1956. Deloris looked up at the new machines and said, "Thank you, thank you, Mr. Seeburg, wherever you are for making our jukebox possible. The new jukeboxes are the thing'. So fancy and not like those ugly wooden things. I'm saving my allowance from babysitting for a 45 rpm Elvis 'rock n' roll."

"How does she know all that stuff?" Asked Emma. Betty

spoke up, "Well, she is the smartest one in our class. You know, the Valedictorian and she reads loads of books."

'Kitty Pearl' lay quietly near all the excitement of jukebox installation. She sees this as a very noisy distraction to her afternoon nap. About that time, KC, Bobby, Peachie and Croz, part of the senior class football team, came parading in. The rest were to follow after getting haircuts at the barber down the street. It seems they did not pass the inspection by Coach McAdams.

"I think Croz is looking for you, Barb. He told Karen he was going to invite you to the 'Sweetheart Dance'. Barb replied, "He better hurry up because I will just go with someone else." 'Kitty Pearl' raised her head. "Really, she's had that dress on layaway since Christmas. I don't see nobody standin' in line. Cruz better hurry up, though, before the last installment is paid, or her brother will be out there bribing someone to take her."

Nila asked Diane, "Do you think Mrs. Jacobson will let the likes of Elvis and his rock' n' roll music in the Daisy Diner blaring from those jukeboxes? You know, being so religious and all?" "She is President of the Methodist Womens Group," Diane said, "All I know is, Mr. Jacobson has not had an empty stool or booth and standing room only since people heard the Daisy Diner was going to do some modernization. Mr and Mrs Jacobson want to keep it old-fashioned but make it family-friendly for teens and such. The employees now have to wear uniforms and those pointy, silly hats. Also, they don't just serve hamburgers, but the new 'breaded tenderloin.' They say it sticks out of the bun. It is so big."

Emma whispered to the girls that Marjorie Major told her Mama that a 'reliable source' told her that by 1958 the jukebox would be replaced. Deloris said, "That stupid party line. Oh, well, by then, we will be graduated, in college and won't be coming into Daisy Diner every day anyway." 'Kitty Pearl' thought, " I can't wait! If those noise boxes are around too long, I'm gonna find me a Diner that serves nothin' but ice cream and plain hamburgers and is closed on Sundays!"

Whether it was by the authority of Marjorie Major or not, the Jukeboxes did not have a long life. Modern technology stepped in.

Chapter Five
Oh! You Wanna Work at the Diner?
You Sure About That Now?

Irene and Eryn were two of the high school Juniors who were selected for The Starlight Diner Trainee Program. Miss Wilson taught high school Home Economics during the school year, and during the last semester of those going into their senior year, girls could apply. Requirements included: A 'C+' grade average, good attendance and no disciplinary actions on record. Little did they know it was almost like attending the very rigid Harvey School of Hospitality.

'Kitty Alfie' said, "Miss Wilson is already called 'Walter' - the Ruler of the Army. Very strict and expects high performance from her students. 'Kitty Alfie' and 'Kitty Luna' marched along beside her each day as she walked from her little cottage to the school and later to The Starlight Diner for training and the final exam, which will be the candidate's first real work day at The Starlight Diner.

"Okay, ladies. Listen up! You will arrive at 7:00 am sharp. You will wear a black skirt that rests below the knee, a white blouse with no ruffles, black socks and shoes. No exceptions. No hair ribbons; hair is to be worn either pulled back in a braid or secured on top of the head. No lip nor cheek color nor painted fingernails.

No jewelry. Any questions?

"No Mam" - the chorus of four all in unison. Each day from three to four, we will commence at the Starlight Diner. The doors will be closed to the public, the shades pulled, and a sign in the window. 'Training Session'.

'Kitty Luna' scooted up to her cousin, 'Kitty Alfie' and said, "Wanna bet 'Blondie', the one over there chompin' her gum like a cow with her cud and acts like she has 'smog in her noggin' won't last the week out." 'Kiitty Alfie' laughed, "I'm thinkin' not all four will be standin' when training class ends. My money goes on the twins!"

"Girls, today we will discuss a most important topic as a Diner employee. Good hygiene and appearance. Everyone in a line, please. I want you to look at each other. Are skirts below the knee, white blouses with no frills, hair appropriate to handling food?" Each looked at each other. No one wanted to say anything. 'Kitty Luna' said, "Get ready." Diane spoke up and said, "Well, Edna is chewing gum, and she has no socks on." Miss Wilson looked at Edna and said, "What say you?" Edna looked at Diane like later she would deal with her, turned to Miss Wilson and said, "My sister wore my only black socks today, and Okay, Okay, I swallowed my gum. If you chew Juicy Fruit gum, your breath will smell good. Never know who you might meet! "Miss Edna!! Tomorrow you will come with black socks or not at all! AND leave the gum at home!"

Miss Wilson looked at the group and said, "We will now proceed without ANY talking. On top of your black skirt and white blouse, you will wear a white apron. Although it will be furnished by The Starlight Diner, you will be responsible for its care. Now, on the table, you will find four white aprons and four pans of water on the Home Economics stoves with a cup of Argo powdered starch in each. You must boil the starch until clear, shut off the pan, let it cool slightly, and dip your apron up and down until fully covered. Then, take it to the clothesline and hang it by the bib. Later, we will iron them to be used as part of your final exam. Remember its importance."

"What if you ain't got no starch? I don't remember seeing any box at my house." "Miss Edna, if you have no starch, you may use sugar. Just boil it until thick. "

"Girls, I suggest you do two aprons at a time. This way, you are prepared for emergencies. Also, polish your shoes at night. Mornings are hectic enough."

"Tomorrow, we will work on Diner Work Ethics 101. Some specifics you will learn through on-the-job training instructed by The Starlight Diner Management staff. Until then, you are dismissed to go home and practice on your aprons." Miss Wilson was exhausted. She looked down at 'Kitty Luna' and said, "Swallow your gum? Who does that?" 'Kitty Luna grinned at 'Kitty Alfie' and said, "Don't think that needs an answer."

Irene and Eryn went through three boxes of Argo starch and six tries. But under the command of their mother's eagle eye, at least two aprons would for sure pass inspection.

"Good morning, today is Work Ethic 101. We will be discussing what makes a 'great' Diner employee. "Eryn, what is the first thing you do when you go to the Diner to work at the start of your shift? "I wash my hands." "Miss Wilson smiled and said, "Correct answer and remember with soap."

Miss Wilson went up to the chalkboard and said, "Now, let's talk some do's and dont's. Many who come into The Starlight Diner regularly are friends or classmates of yours. She wrote: At no time do you stop your counter service to lean over and chat. At no time do you give free food or fountain drinks? At no time do you encourage your unpaying friends to 'hang out'. This will result in immediate termination."

Edna came to life. "Yep, and don't mess with those regulars, the Booker boys caus' they are greasers, ya know. That one dude, Jaylo, is annoying. He's a senior and thinks that gives him privileges, but I heard my buddy Harger tell him he was 'cruisin' for a bruisin' if he messed with him. Don't give him free nothin'." 'Kitty Alfie' rolled over laughing. "I'm thinking 'Blondie' has a lot of experience. Just not sure it will pass the 'work at the Diner' test."

Miss Wilson thanked Edna for her input. "Let's continue. Never get into a confrontation with a customer. They are always right even when they are not. Call the manager over. And, there never is to be an empty coffee cup at the counter. This is a trademark of all Diners..always served with a smile. Finally, have fun!"

Miss Wilson smiled over her little, narrow glasses and said, "Next Friday, you are to arrive in full dress at The Starlight Diner at 3:00 - final exam day. You know what to do - Now do it!"

Two girls in full uniform with perfectly starched uniforms, hair braided, and no make-up arrived on time, and Miss Wilson could not be more proud. "They COULD pass the Harvey Girl School of Hospitality."

'Kitty Alfie' and 'Kitty Luna' declared they 'were best in class - Junior class that is'.

'Kitty Luna' was napping but overheard a conversation between Edna and Miss Wilson. "What's wrong with chewing gum? You can always swallow it! And, put my hair up on my head! Wear a skirt below my knees! Really? This is 1956. Who cares what you wear in a Diner? And I am not going to cow-tow to a bunch of ankle biters who come in for ice cream cones and dribble it all over. I bet they don't even leave a tip!"

The Starlight Diner giggled as 'Kitty Alfie' and 'Kitty Luna' heard Edna going out the door mumbling something about working at her Uncle John's gas station. Her friend, Mary, said her boyfriend didn't want her working all spiffed up at a Diner where boys would be hangin' out! So, down to two. Two good ones.

The twins, Irene and Eryn, worked at The Starlight Diner part-time through their senior year and full-time during the summers. They were recipients of the Starlight Diner scholarship to attend college. Both attended and graduated from DePaul University and returned to teach high school Home Economics, which included the Diner Intern Program.

'Kitty Alfie' won the bet. His money was on The Twins.

Chapter Six
Wimpy's Diner - An Institution

Whitney Wiley Martin. Pretty big name for a baby. Later, shortened to Wimpy, he looked over at Lola, his wife and best friend, and as he looked out of the backyard window, remarked, "We have been in the eatery business for years. I, as you know, have wanted to do something different. An off-the-wall place where men in their overalls are as comfortable as the local National Bank President in his 3-piece suit." Lola stopped what she was doing and inquired softly, "What is it you want to do?" "Well, if we could open a small Diner, we would never change the recipe nor allow anyone else to change it! Simple, honest burgers, coney dogs and the most memorable chili in America. Along with your pies, of course. We already know they will be talked about for generations to come." Lola laughed and said, "And we should call it 'Wimpy's Diner'.

'Wimpy' said, "You know I saw an old beat-up trolley car, and there was a little sign in the window. 'For sale - best offer'." 'Kitty Felix', the orphaned cat, dropped in front of the house in a box and said, "From the looks of it, not too many people will be making an offer. Should ask if you can haul it to the dump for free." 'Wimpy' said out loud, "It would be perfect, but getting it to our little location may be the biggee!"

We've been hearing about 'lunch cars' for a while, but I want something more unique." Lola grinned, "Just like you, Wimpy."

Later that day, Lola sat in her rocking chair with 'Kitty Felix' on her lap. "I'm a bit concerned. Wimpy, do you think we can make it work right in the middle of a Depression? "We will, sweet Lola, and I'll tell you why." 'Kitty Felix' looked up and thought, "This better be good." We will sell two Wimpy burgers for 15 cents. No frills. Just hot off the grill, delicious special recipe, big burgers. And introduce a 'chili bowl' that no small Diner has around these parts. A bonus: fresh, right-out-the-oven fruit pies. Ample piece for 5 cents. We will stay open longer to accommodate the second shift automaker employees, who can slip over for a hot 'chili bowl' that will be cheaper than packing a little black lunch box. Free coffee for the regulars.

Time marches on - new generations arrive, but some things never change. "Wimpy's Diner," for one.

The little silver trolly still stands in the same place with the well-used 'ole greasy spoon' grill up front in full view. Autoworkers working on the newest generations of cars, soldiers leaving for war and returning out of harm's way, and young people who follow in their parent's footsteps all still come in to find an empty, well-worn stool at 'Wimpy's Diner' counter.

The elder 'Kitty Felix', who was the official greeter for many years, has now retired to his fluffy pillow and can be seen most days by the pie cabinet. He still observes the locals, and new returning soldiers but lets 'Kitty Felix II' handle the day-to-day at 'Wimpy's Diner'. He, like his father, so enjoys the young people, who in family tradition, treat Wimpy's Chili Bowl like a staple. Often using their own allowance.

Lola has trained two generations of Wimpy employees. Some say, Charlie, Maydee and Jose have been there twenty years or more. Lola has not relinquished her pie-making secrets yet, but talks of training a pie maker 'one of these days'. 'Kitty Felix' says, "Yea, about like she and Wimpy talk about 'hangin' it up'. Someday."

Lola looked up from her rolling pin and said, "Hi KAB, you're running a little late today, aren't you? "Well, Miss Lola, I tore my shirt, climbing over the fence. I only have ten minutes to eat my chili bowl, or they will close the playground door, and I can't slip back in." Miss Lola told him to take off his shirt, and she would stitch up the small tear so it would not be noticeable. "Miss Lola, my teacher asked me what or where I ate my lunch since we were not allowed to leave campus. I told her my grandma made me a meatloaf sandwich. Thank goodness that's not true since I hate those things. Speaking of grandma's, Miss Lola. My grandpa and grandma are visiting from Kentucky. Grandpa doesn't talk much, but Grandma is a real trip. She told me if she heard me say 'dang it' again or wood cussed (means slam the door) again, she was going to wash my mouth out with soap. Miss Lola, I know I charge my 'chili bowl' to Dad's work account, and I didn't ask him if I could. You see, Campy, my friend whose Dad is the Police Chief, does it, so I got the idea from him. But, if Grandma found out, do you think she would scrape the soap over my teeth? She told my two brothers she was going to do that to them?"

Miss Lola looked at the sweet boy standing in front of her. "Well, KAB, you know skipping over the school fence and not asking permission to charge your food is wrong. Tell you what I am going to do. I have not charged your dad's account for three 'chili bowls' and one 'Wimpy' burger. If you come in Saturday morning and help 'Wimpy' clean the grill and other chores, your debt will be paid but no more fibbing. Understand?" KAB looked shocked. "Clean the grill? Why I heard "Wimpy's Grill" was called 'ye ole greasy spoon' because Wimpy never, ever cleaned his grill, and that's why the hamburgers were so awesome." Miss Lola giggled. "Well, KAB, the truth is Wimpy wants people to think that. That's part of his secret recipe. The real truth is on Saturday before opening, he pulls out a BIG scraper/brush and cleans the grill. I think you could help keep his secret by cleaning the grill on Saturday morning. I am pretty sure he could be convinced you might have all the hamburgers and 'chili bowls' you might want. Another secret among us! Is that a deal?" KAB grinned. "Miss Lola, would you tell Wimpy I will see him Saturday morning."

KAB's father thought helping Wimpy was a good idea. And KAB felt ever grateful that grandma never had to exercise the soap threat. KAB became a fixture and worked throughout high school. He never told his brothers that each work Saturday, there was a piece of freshly baked pie with a little card. "Don't touch - KAB's." His official title was "pie sampler".

KAB wasn't keen on college right after high school, so when Wimpy and Lola offered (IF he took an accounting class so he could help with Lola's bookkeeping) a full-time position as Wimpy's Diner Assistant Manager, he could not wait. He even got a hat with a big 'W' on it.

Ye ole' greasy spoon secret, the recipes, and Lola's pie secret will, as 'Wimpy' says, "Go to the grave with us."

Over the years, KAB always said to 'Kitty Felix', "One could say they had the recipe for success in more ways than one."

Chapter Seven
Hey Joe, Can I Use Your Diner for .....

It's the start of a new week, and the phone is already ringing at Joe's Diner. As usual, Joe answered, "DINER, Joe speaking", a man of few words.

"Hey Joe, it's Earl Sands, Councilman, 5th District. You know, I'm thinkin' it'd be good for you small business owners to have me give my final speech before the election at your Diner. I have a lot of influence, you know. Sure could throw a lot of business your way." Joe replied, "Have to get back with ya. What's your name - Earl?" 'Kitty Chil' started giggling. "That blowhard couldn't throw a baseball to first place, much less throw business 'our way'." The Diner said, "And I can count the stools on one hand he has sat on to help this small business owner."

Joe, 'Kitty Chil' and the Diner decided that would be a 'no' vote.

Just can't turn the cutest little cheerleaders on the planet, whispered The Diner. Here they come.

"Hi, Mr. Joe. We are Melissa, Marian and Martha, and we are going to be cheerleaders for the new Wayne High School this coming year. We came with an offer! Since the school has no money for uniforms or equipment, we have to fund raise ourselves. So, we thought if we could put a big glass jar with our flyer pasted on the front up by the register, maybe people would drop their change in there. But that's not all. If you would let us, we would dress in jeans and 'Joe's Diner' shirts and work for free each Saturday in August. We would do any kind of work you need done. If the customers see us working, they might just put change in the jar."

'Kitty Chil' and The Diner looked at each other, smiling. "Well, if that don't take all. That's a no-brainer. Besides that, they are so cute - and that can't hurt business. When do they start?"

Ole' rough talkin' Joe , we are told, slipped a $100 bill in the jar. Also, on the opening Friday night game, the girls dressed in new cheerleading outfits waved at their friends, Mr Joe and 'Kitty Chil', who sat on the 50-yard line. Seems they are the cheerleaders 'best' cheerleaders.

Mrs. Gerten, Community Church President, Community Action Council President, and Community Women's Library Council President, came into the Diner on Wednesday with two very fancy dressed ladies. All three wore 'plumy' hats with feathers that looked freshly plucked. So, 'Kitty Chi' noticed. "Jumpin' Jehoshaphat, she looks like she has some real important business to talk to Joe. 'Kitty Chi' leaned up against Joe Diner's cooler, hoping the intrusion of non-paying society ladies might just be cut short. The Diner said, "Wrong, she is sitting down. That means she wants something." "Hi, Joe!" Using all her feminine wiles hoping to get him to agree to her demands of the day. "Ladies, how can I help you?" "We represent the Society of Equality for the Rights of

Women in the Greater Wayne County." We would like to set up a booth in front of The Diner - in the street, of course - at the upcoming Labor Day Rally."

'Kitty Chili' jumped up and shook his head. "What kind of silly Society is that? That lady has her nose in way too much now!" The Diner said, "We better distance ourselves from all that flag waivin' stuff, megaphone blowin' right in front of The Diner. Who wants to eat lunch listenin' to that noise!" "Joe said, "I'll have to get back to ya."

'Kitty Chil" looked at Joe's Diner and said, "Well, that would be a no! But, perhaps - in the street, of course - way down the street, of course!"

The Joe's Diner supported the United Mine Workers of America. The miners frequently came into the Diner, and Joe listened compassionately to the issues miners faced daily. He did not advertise, but the local Union meetings were often held after hours at the banquet table.

"Joe, we are here to tell you next month John L Lewis, the President of the United Mine Workers, will be here for a surprise visit. He works tirelessly to defeat the radical insurgents who want to control the Union. He wants to talk about wage and benefit increases for miners and to explain his support for the first Federal Mine Safety Act. 'Kitty Chili's' voice elevated. "Did you just hear the local Mine President ask Joe to have the big meeting right here in your "Joe's Diner"?

The Joe's Diner smiled and said, "It goes without saying - that will be a YES!"

The sign on the door said

The Joe's Diner

CLOSED

To Outside Events

Until Further Notice

Chapter Eight
Hatch Chile Milkshakes!!
And How Many of Those You Gonna Sell?

The 66 Diner patiently waits for this year's crop of Hatch Chiles to fully ripen. It's been almost 85 days, it's September, and the Hatch Chile harvest in New Mexico is in full swing.

Pepe' Garcia has run The 66 Diner since it opened. Each year, he says the same thing. "We need to do something different this year to remain competitive.

'Kitty Karmelita' looked at her friend, '66' she called her and said, "I think Pepe' has lost some gray matter up there. Who in their right mind is going to drink a Hatch Chile milkshake? '66' laughed. "Sit by, wait and watch! Remember last year? The meanest Hatch Chile chili soup known to man was the featured item on the menu. Truckers are still carrying Milk of Magnesia in their glove boxes. I know it's going to be a banner season. The old cooler that sits by the door is going to be full and overflowing with Hatch Chiles. The smell will hit the customers the minute they open the door. By the way, the word is already getting out to the locals. So, get ready!

'Kitty Karmelita' was lying under the table listening to the employees talking at their weekly meeting. Pepe' said, "We have to be different. There are many Diners along Route 66, and we need to make ours a 'destination'. Throw out all your ideas, and remember there are no bad ones." Let's take advantage of our bigger-than-normal Hatch Chile crop."

The long-time employees knew they were valued, and they would be the ones formulating and tweaking the recipes.

Huerte popped up. "What about taking a plain hamburger and slicing the chile very thin on top and then grilling them together."

Maria, the head cook, said, "Let's chop the Hatch Chiles with other veggies, slice a pocket in a pork chop, and bake it. Serve with a small bowl of '66's chili."

Roberto quietly said, "I brought this up earlier but you want different. Let's make a Hatch Chile Milkshake. Use vanilla ice cream, a little agave, and cleaned, no skin, no seeds Hatch Chiles so it won't be too hot." Put a sign out front.

BEST HATCH CHILE VANILLA MILKSHAKES ON 'ROUTE 66!

Pepe', 'Kitty Karmelita' and '66 Diner smiled and decided ALL ideas would be used. "Like I said, no bad ideas."

The ice cream truck driver could not believe his ears. He asked, "How much vanilla ice cream you ordering? "You heard me, Pepe' said. "But that's triple what you usually get!." "YUP, it sure is!

Trucker Manfred, coming through on his way to California, said, "Nobody, but nobody is going to believe me when I tell them I drank a Hatch Chile Vanilla Milkshake on Route 66 at the '66 Diner'.

It was a banner year, indeed!

Chapter Nine
My Forever Friend is Back!
Mama, Can I Go to the Dandy Diner?

Grandpa Johnson told his wife, Nelda, he was going to the Paw Paw patches today down by the railroad track. Now abandoned, he no longer worries about the little children, Bruno, the bodyguard dog and 'Kitty Manxy' running into harm's way.

"I thought I would go pick up Andy Brins and her friend Blacki to go with me. I'll give each of them a gunny sack. It's a great day for picking all sorts of berries. We will donate them to the Dandy Diner for his milkshakes. I'll stop by and tell Graden and Walter so they will know the kids will be spending Saturday with me.

The two, almost nine year olds, were so excited to once more share a creamy milkshake. This time, it was a fresh strawberry and as always, delicious. Equally as excited to go 'way down yonder in the paw paw patch' with Grandpa Johnson.

"Grandpa Johnson is not really my grandpa. I just call him that. Seems he is a friend of my mom's. At church, I have to call Mr. and Mrs. Bays, Sister Bays and Brother Bays, and everyone else older than dirt. But they aren't my sister or brother either. Seems a bit dumb to me."

Blacki laughed, picked up the gunny sacks, and they trotted along behind Grandpa Johnson. "How you likin' that church school over in Frankfort?," Grandpa asked. Blacki looked up from skipping over the wood planks and said, "I don't! Those people should take 'Learn to Smile 101'. Not allowed to talk to anybody. Bed is hard as a rock. Can't play ball. I figure one day, I'll stir up some excitement when the headmaster isn't looking. Have to be careful. My dad is a real, what they call ordained preacher now. It means he will get his own church, and will go preach at other churches sometimes. I want to be here, go to school with my friends like Andy."

"Who made paw paws, and what do we do with them?" asked Andy. "Well, God made them. They are a custard-like fruit. Only pick up the ones that are dark and on the ground. Green ones taste sour. Miss Nelda makes Paw Paw nut bread. Mighty tasty. She wants to freeze some for the upcoming church bake sale. Also, let's see how many berries we can find. We will give them to Dandy Diner. Guess who just might get a berry milkshake smiled Grandpa Johnson."

"Blacki, do you think you will ever be able to come back here, go to school and play football with our friends, KC and Crozier?"

Blacki replied, "Well, if my plan works, I will. KC and I have a plan. When we get a little older, we can work on the big Conner Farm. If I can show Mom and Dad that I can make some money and help them, they might let me out of that Church prison camp. Don't call it that, or we both might get in trouble."

"Grandpa, me and Blacki have gobs of pawpaws and almost a full bucket of berries. Boy, time flies when you are having fun." Grandpa Johnson loved every moment of having little Andy around. He often wished he could be in Graden and Claras' shoes and be her real grandpa. Adopted or not.

"Bruno, 'Kitty Manxy', let's get the kids back to the Diner. Still have time for a milkshake."

Chapter Ten

The Nook #2 Diner at the Depot - A Wedding at the Diner?

As part of the Whistle Stop Depot, The Nook #2 Diner nestles right up against The Depot. It allows people coming off the train a break from the screeching of trains carrying mostly soldiers to war and get a great hamburger with a free cup of coffee. 'Kitty Sarge,' the official greeter of the young soldiers, who have never been out of their state, much less out of the country, said," In fact, the coffee makers wear out faster than the news ones can get here from Indianapolis. 'Kitty Sarge' ain't my real name. Just thinkin' the soldiers might like it better than 'Kitty Katch'. My real job is to catch critters and keep them out of the Depot/Diner."

Most soldiers this month have been recently drafted with little notice to change their life's plans. The new recruits receive an official written notice with a date on it to report to Fort Benjamin Harrison for training. Some will be going to Military Police Corp School, Finance School, Chaplain School and even Music School. They don't know it yet. The tests given in the first week of official induction will determine where the Army needs you to be. 'Kitty Sarge' grinned at the thought. " Not sure they will be given a lot of choice. I bet there will be a lot of potato peelers, pan scrubbers and floor washers."

The Nook #2 Diner has seen it all. The food has to be simple and the coffee hot. He told 'Kitty Sarge', "The trains don't wait on long, sit-down meals. 'Kitty Sarge' shouted, "OR long kissy face goodbyes' for that matter. By the way, I see several local boys hardly out of high school in this last month's recruitment."

The Nook #2 said, "One of them is Dennis O'Hara. Doubt he has been far from the farm. Since they had to register at eighteen for the draft, it did not take long for them to cast a net across the entire Midwest. In fact, some of our travelers told me that the Army recruiters went way down in the deep woods of the Appalachian Mountains and drafted fifty young men at a time." 'Kitty Sarge' said, "Well, Let me tell you, there is no better than Dennis O'Hara to take a tractor, combine, truck or anything else that moves on wheels apart, fix it and put it back together again. If they don't put him in the Army Wheeled Vehicle Mechanic Unit, they got marbles for brains."

Bill Gerard, the son of George and Mary Gerard, the local Accountant, received his draft papers this week. His plans were to join his father in the Accounting Office. "Father, what am I going to do? You know Saturday, Alice Hubbart and I are to be married in the Friends Church. She is wearing her mother's wedding dress and grandmother's veil. And, her Aunt Ginny is making the two-tiered wedding cake. We already have our license. It would be like leaving her at the altar. My train to Fort Benjamin Harrison leaves at 9:10."

Mary Gerard said, "I have an idea. Since time is the issue, let me talk to my friend, Depot #3 Ticketmaster and see if we could just move the vows portion performed by the Army Chaplain with Alice and Bill and families into the Depot. Then, take the flowers and Aunt Ginny's two-tier wedding cake into the Nook #2 Diner with coffee and iced tea. We could celebrate until the train comes." "Oh, Mother, would you?" said Alice, tearing up. "You just go get ready."

Something old - mother's dress. Something new - her little white shoes. Something borrowed - Bills' mother's handkerchief and something blue - the garter the girls all gave her at her wedding shower. 'Kitty Sarge' said, "Ain't she the prettiest thing."

At 6:30 in the Depot, Alice Hubbart became Mrs. Bill Girard in her mother's dress, grandmother's veil and a small bouquet of flowers. At 6:50, they were joined in the Nook #2 Diner for the cutting of Aunt Ginny's two-tier wedding cake. At 8:30, the couple said their goodbyes, thanked everyone for coming and went out on the railroad benches to say some words of endearment.

At 9:30, the Interurban Train at C.W. Station whistle could be heard but not over the crying of many mothers, wives and girlfriends wondering and praying that the war might end soon and bring ALL the boys home safely.

Chapter Eleven
Let's Make a Beeline to the Beeline Diner!

"I ain't goin' to that Beeline Diner. No Way!" yelled Charlie Avery. His brother, Chilton, looked fondly down at his brother, who looked at things often through a different lens and said, "Why so, Charlie?" "Well, don't you remember when I went to Aunt Laura's big white houses where the bees live, and all I did was take my finger and lick some honey and all of a sudden, a big ole' bee came up and bit me on the lip? My face swelled up awful." 'Kitty Kranley' stuck his head up out of the bike basket. He was waiting for his ride down to the Beeline Diner. "Charlie gets in a few places he best not be. Thank goodness he has his brother Chilton. Come on, guys, it's Friday night. I'm hungry."

"Come on, Charlie, It's a Diner. They don't serve bees 'on a bun'. It's a Friday night fish fry. Fresh cod, to be exact." Charlie hesitated and then said, "Well, my friend, Harlos, he told me that they dipped bees in whiskey, and it would make me smart if I ate a bunch of them 'cause I am so dumb." Chilton put his arm around his younger brother and spoke quietly. "You aren't dumb, Charlie. You are special in a lot of ways. You know where to find frogs in the creek, and we have a good frog leg dinner that night now don't we? And besides that, 'beeline' just means we will go straight and fast to the Diner. I will deal with Harlos later. Now get your shoes and socks on, and don't forget your suspenders." 'Kitty Kranley' shouted, "I'm dying here. Starving to death here. Does anyone care?"

"You know who we might see tonight, Charlie? Zane Gray, the writer of all those zillions of books. I heard the ladies at the church say he was moving up here. He writes about cowboys and all sorts of other stuff." "But, Chilton, where does he find all those zillion words to put in his zillion books? Can you teach me some so I can know about cowboys, too? You taught me how to tie my shoes and put my shirt on frontwards." Chilten loved his brother so much, but there were just some things he could not teach him or have all the answers. Since their mother took off with the traveling Watkins vanilla salesman to an exciting life rather than being stuck with a 'dumb' kid and a dad who can't stay away from the moonshine stills in the mountains, Chilton has been responsible for his 'special' brother, Charlie.

'Kitty Kranley', Charlie and Chilton consumed a large part of the weekly cod catch with the 'all you can eat' Friday night special.

A few months later, Chilton asked Charlie if he might like to go to school. A school where they did not make fun of him or take his glasses off and stomp on them. 'Kitty Kranley' thought, "I better listen in on this because the school here on the mountain didn't do no good for Charlie." "Can you and 'Kitty Kranley' go too?" asked Charlie. "We will see about that, but what they are telling me is they are bringing in a 'very special' teacher. You know her. It's Miss

Granger, who works at the Beeline Diner. She just graduated from a college that makes you a 'Special Education' teacher. You will ride a special bus, and even though you go to the school on the hill, you won't be going to the same classes with the likes of Harlo." 'Kitty Kranley' said, "I still will deal with him one day."

"Where will I sleep, Chilton?" "You will come home on the same bus and sleep in your own bed." "Will she teach me how to read Zane Gray cowboy books and big words like Beeline? His brother said, "Charlie, you are going to learn so many things. You will be smarter than Harlo." Charlie grinned and said, 'Kitty Kranley', "Maybe we will just feed Harlo some bees dipped in whiskey."

Charlie is smarter than you think!

Chapter Twelve
Mama, Listen to Me.
My Forever Friend is Going to Go to Our High School. For Sure!

Kenny yelled across the Study Hall, "Meet me at the Dandy Diner after school. I got something I got to tell ya!."

Andy arrived and quickly told her best friend she was in a hurry because she needed to get home, do her household chores and get right to her homework. "Well, do I have news for you!! Blacki's parents gave up on the Church Boarding School, and they are bringing Blacki home. He will not only go to our high school but will play football and baseball with our team. The Church School was going to kick him out anyway. You see, he called the Town Fire Department and told them there was a man on the roof and couldn't get down. He knew that because he had put him out there through a window and then locked it so he could not get back in."

Bruno and 'Kitty Manxy 'said, "His mother is madder than a smacked hornet's nest. Wait until he sees the list of 'things HE cannot do!' Breathe might be a close #1. He will be in the penalty box for a while. Mrs. Blac don't mess around."

"Kenny, whatever you do, don't mention this to anyone who might tell my Mom, or she won't let me see Blacki for the rest of my life." "Gotcha covered, little girl", the name he often called her even when she became old.

Andy went with her Mom to the farm that weekend. As usual, she found her Grandad in the barn, her favorite place. She sat next to him on another stool and said, "I have a secret." She then told him why Blacki wouldn't be going back to the Boarding School. He started laughing so loud that Ole' Bessie turned her head to see what the ruckus was during the milking. He said, "They should have done something with that Boarding School a long time ago. Boys need sports and fun things to do. No wonder they were always up to something."

"Have you told your Mom yet?" "Not yet."

Later, after Andy had completed her chores, she casually mentioned Kenny had told her Blacki was coming home to live with his parents instead of going back to the Boarding School. No explanation was given, "He's going to play football and..." she was interrupted. Her Mom quickly said, "YOU are going to be a Senior soon, and the ONLY thing you should be thinking about is making A's in your classes, being on the Honor Roll and getting scholarships for college. The reason we moved back from the farm is because you need to learn more than bailing hay, fixing tractors, canning Ball jars. If your grades fall one bit, you won't be going out of the house, much less going to some silly football game. Do you understand me?" "Yes, Mam."

Summer jobs ended, school started, football practice had begun, and the Class of '57 was on its way. Andy did not see much of Blacki or Kenny, but they plotted regularly to meet in the school library. When Coach McAny asked for volunteers to tutor his athletes in Civics and Government, a graduation requirement, Andy quickly raised her hand. She loved History and won the contest for knowing the most answers on the Constitution. So, her study hall period was now in the library as a tutor.

Sure enough, the new football fullback was in attendance. Later, during Commencement, Principal Stuart jokingly said, "Andy Brins really should get three diplomas. Blacki and Kenny passed Civics and Government due to her tutoring." Andy blushed as the football team cheered.

Since Reverend and Mrs. Blac traveled around to 'revivals' - some in white tents, others in little towns that were hard to pronounce like Swayzee and Montpelier. Blacki asked his parents if Andy could go with them on Saturday night. The answer: "Ask her Mother." When Blacki told Andy, she replied, "We know what that answer will be."

Blacki went to the Daisy Diner, where Andy's Mom worked. He waited until it seemed she was not real busy and asked, "Miss Brins, Can Andy go to a church revival with me and my Mother and Father on Saturday night? She has never heard my dad preach. It's not a date or nothing." After what seemed like a year, she said, "Well, I suppose, but they need to pick her up and drop her off. I don't have time to be a delivery service!" "YES MAM! He got out of there before she had a chance to change her mind.

The next day after church, when Andy and her mom went to the farm, Andy went to the barn where her Grandad was working on a tractor. She said, "Grandad, guess what? Mom let me go to a revival last night with Reverend Blac, Mrs. Blac and Blacki." "How did that go?" "Now, don't tell Granny or Mom, but Blacki reached over and held my hand on the way back from the revival. His mother was talking a lot about people getting saved and stuff like that." "Andy, just keep your grades up. I can't help you if they fall." "I know, Grandad" "Did you have fun?" Andy grinned. "You know I did, and ran over for a big hug."

Graduation came around quickly. Blacki received numerous football and baseball invitations with scholarships. At least Eastern Illinois University's offer with a full ride wasn't as far away as Dartmouth. Andy was expected to go to her Church of God College twenty miles away. She could come home on weekends and work at the shoe store. Her scholarships barely covered a semester since private colleges were much more expensive. She and Blacki had saved all their change in glass jars. But, even after counting, rolling, wrapping and putting in shoeboxes, it would hardly cover Andys' meal ticket for the semester, much less anything left over to buy things for her cedar-lined hope chest. Working full-time throughout the summer would help, and her church family would help, too. Grandad told her not to worry; things would work out.

It was late August. The Class of '57 was packing for the next chapter of their lives. Some joining the Armed Services, some are heading to college and others are already married and starting their new lives.

Blacki had worked at the Conner Farm all summer and had saved some extra by working on Saturdays. He called Andy and said, "Meet me at the Dandy Diner about 3:00 o'clock on Saturday, okay?" Andy thought for sure Blacki was going to tell her he had to go to the University, and they should no longer go steady. She was determined not to break into tears. 'Kitty Manxy ' jumped up on Andy's lap. She knew Andy would be devastated if she got that sort of news.

Blacki had gone home and changed out of his farm overalls and work shoes. He walked into the Diner, and when he saw Andy already perched on a stool, he thought, " I am looking at the prettiest and smartest girl I have ever met in my whole life. 'Kitty Manxy' thought, "He is so handsome. What a hunk!" He sat down on the stool she had saved for him. Looking at Andy, he said, "Well, Kenny told me I was an insensitive idiot for not telling you how I felt before I left for the University. SO! I'm going to tell you I don't want to go steady anymore. You can keep my class ring if you like since it does not fit me. But would you wear this ring instead and be engaged?" 'Kitty Manxy ' jumped up and ran out to tell Bruno. Andy opened a little white box to see the most beautiful engagement ring she could have ever wanted. 'Kitty Manxy ' jumped up and peered in the tiny box. "Now that boy is a keeper!" BRUNO, wake up. This is important stuff."

Blacki kissed Andy on the forehead and said, "I still want to be your forever friend.

Chapter Thirteen
It's Still a Diner. Just the Walk-Up Kind

"Wyoming is magnificent, and just look at all the plentiful fresh meat," said Johney Clover to his brother, Juster. Juster frowned, "What ya gonna do, have people chase us down the road?"

"Juster, hear me out now! Johney Clover wanted to state his case in hopes his brother might just stay in Wyoming with them. Johney and his wife, Ruth, had a reputation for being very nomadic. They preferred to roam rather than have roots in one spot of brick-and-mortar. They had no children. Just their beloved cat, 'Kitty Echo'.

"Grandpa Clover put in his will that we were to receive his old 'roach coach,' he called it. Everything works. Why not paint it silver, trim it in red like a Diner, and call it The Clover Diner? We could have three drop-down diner stools with red diner-style seats in front, and when we stop, put out a couple of tables with red checkered tablecloths. Finally, a BIG sign that says "The Best Bison, Bear, Antelope and Elk Burgers in the West!" "What do you guys think?"

Ruth looked at 'Kitty Echo' and said, "Here we go again! My dear, little tuxitude with your moustache that twitches when you smile. It's a good thing you are so easygoing and go along with our 'drop and roll lifestyle."

'Kitty Echo' looked across the vast Wyoming landscape and thought this had to be the biggest place he had ever been. Tall mountains, big parks, BIG animals and not very many people. Hoping those visitors come through like odd hamburgers. "Miss Ruth, way back when, my forefathers were part of the Spanish Empire in Wyoming. Being Latino and all, I guess it won't be too bad of a place to be. But I have a question. So we get this Diner thing moving down the road. How you gonna get Bison, Elk, Antelope and Deer between a bun?" Ruth laughed hysterically. "Good question, 'Kitty Echo'. Good question. That's one for the Clover boys."

With everyone buying into the project, The Clover Walk-Up Diner was in business. By spring, they were traveling where the action was anywhere in the state. 'Kitty Echo' told his friend, Clover Diner, that he was a Tuxedo cat, not a cowboy cat, but he sure liked going where those pretty ladies and gents did the 'Swing Dances' because the feline attendees thought he was very dashing and charming. You know, with my black and white tuxedo. The Clover Diner looked down at his rather conceited friend and said, "You may have come from the Spanish Empire, but you still can't walk on water."

Before long, The Clover Diner had a reputation for being the best 'on wheels walk-up Diner' anywhere and was worth 'catching up to'. 'Kitty Echo' told The Clover Diner, "You know my friend, 'Kitty Roderick' climbed Mt. Everest, but I am happy just roaming all over Wyoming. I still am not sure how those big animals make it inside that little bun."

The Clover Diner laughed and said, "When I get a minute, I'll tell you our little secret!"

Chapter Fourteen
Times are a Changin'. Want a Hamburger and Cherry Pie and Listen to Rock n Roll? You Can Still Go to the Diner - Maybe.

'Kitty Ailba Dillon' was shaking off the rain in her long coat full of the morning rain. She ran to lay near the hamburger grill, which was always on and warm. It's pouring down rain with thunder and lightning and driving people into the Dublin Diner from the street outside.

'Kitty A', she was called by staff, said: "Hi Moses, sure wet out there." Moses Win was in the back washing dishes and cleaning the kitchen area. Moses was the first negro hired to work inside Peter O'Donnel's Dublin Diner. He felt honored and grateful, and no dish would leave his kitchen without being spotless. His cousin, Madee, made the best cherry pie in the South, and worked three days a week keeping the pie cabinet full. 'Kitty A' always listened to the Dublin Diner chatter while it continued to pour buckets of rain. No one inside the Diner was moving except to be in line for a coffee or maybe Madee's pie.

Jimal Buckner was heading to the gas station to get his bike tire filled with air when the storm came out of nowhere with a vengeance. He, like many others, jumped into the Dublin Diner to get out of the downpour and got in line to get a hot chocolate to take out. He was dripping wet and getting colder by the minute. He saw a familiar face. "Hi, Moses' How's it goin'?" Moses looked up to see his Pastors' son, Jamal in line. "Good, see you in church Sunday." "Yes, Sir."

All of a sudden, it was very quiet. A black boy was in line to get a hot chocolate. "Hey, you. Boy, you need to get yourself outa here. You can't eat in here!" The BIG man started taking off his belt. Peter O'Donnel came out quickly from the grill where he was flippin' hamburgers. 'Kitty Ailba Dillon,' appropriately named for white lightning, came flying around the corner at the same time. Both got between the man and Jamal.

"This is my Diner. I moved here years ago from Ireland because of constant fighting between Protestants and Catholics. People were needlessly killing each other. The aftermath was worse than the potato famine. I will say who can or cannot work here OR eat here. I know Jamal. He delivers our fresh fruit and vegetables in his bike basket every day. Now leave him alone and get out!!" "Madee, would you fix Jamal a hot chocolate in a take-out cup so he can go get his tire fixed." "Yes, sir. Madee quickly filled the cup and put a little extra foam on top before placing a tight lid. Jamal bowed and said, "Thank you Mam. God Bless." He looked at Peter O'Donnel, the proud owner of The Dublin Diner and grinned the biggest grin ever!

In 1964, President Lyndon B. Johnson signed the Civil Rights

Act. The Supreme Court ended segregation in restaurants.

Even today, many Diners only serve take-outs to black customers.

Some say, "That's just the way it is."

Chapter Fifteen
Not Just a 'Forever Friend'

Blacki looked across the room where Andy was getting dressed. "Does this sweater look okay?" Andy smiled, "You look great. Handsome as usual. Seventy years of marriage looks good on you." "Well, you are still the prettiest and smartest girl I have ever known." Andy laughed, "Flattery will always get you somewhere! Are you ready to head to the Dandy Diner? The 5K's no doubt are already there and others as well by now."

Blacki said, "Unfortunately, Bruno and 'Kitty Manxy' won't be with us, but they no doubt are saying "Have a scoop of ice cream for us."

The Dandy Diner still stands on the same corner. Two generations of serving ice cream sodas and milkshakes at the same old fountain. A part or two has had to be replaced along the way, but it still purs along. The counter stools look the same, but over the years, they, too, have had to have a little spiffing with a red seat recover or two.

As they walked the short distance from their little cottage on Logan Street, Blacki asked, "Do you remember nearly 75 years ago when Mother sent me, Bruno and 'Kitty Manxy' to take you to the Dandy Diner for a soda?"

"Well, I remember what you said when you guys walked me to my house," Andy grinned. "Me, too."

The Diner door opened, and Uncle Harlo's son, Harold, had lined up all along the counter old 1950s soda glasses. Uncle Harlo had been driven from his home to dip the first ice cream scoop to put in his nephew, Blacki and Andys' glass. At ninety, he said he would not miss this for anything in the world. A vintage soda glass sat in the center with two straws surrounded by a small wreath of red roses. The glass had 'Happy 70 Years" written on the side. All 5K's, KC and their parents sat up at The Dandy Diner sipping an ice cream soda nearly 75 years after the very first time. Blacki said, "Uncle Harlo, remember how I brought an extra dime for Andy's ice cream because she didn't have any money, and over the years, you figured out ways we could 'work off' our sodas? He reached down, pulled out his billfold and pulled out a small picture of Andy. On the back, he had taped the dime. "I carried this for 70+ years just in case you ever asked for her to pay." Everyone roared laughing, including Uncle Harlo. "If she ever stopped being your Forever Friend, believe me, I would have collected that dime," grinned his adoring Uncle.

KLB said, "Father, Mother, we aren't done yet." About that time, a black limo drove up. Blacki asked, "Where are we going? "Oh! You'll see. Now let's go."

As they began to drive, it became clear where they were going. The 5K's and KC had worked on this surpise for a year. All of a sudden, the limo stopped. At the entrance to the lane, a huge, beautifully designed sign welcomed them, "THE BLACK FAMILY FOREVER HOME AND SCHOOL FOR PERFECT CHILDREN."

As they drove down the long, maple tree-lined lane, in the yard were over 200 people. Blacki and Andy were in awe. As the limo stopped, they saw over 100 children, now adults, who had passed through the current Forever Home and School. Another hundred family members, including eleven of the most beautiful grandchildren in the world and community members stood all over the porch and lawn. Andy said, "Wow, what a well-kept surprise, and Oh! my goodness, look at my farmhouse!!

KJB, the family Contractor, had been busy remodeling and outfitting the beautiful old farmhouse and barn Andy's grandad had willed to her when he passed. "Grandad said, "Andy, take your farmhouse and barn and do what you always do. Continue to make it be alive for the good of others." The current little Forever Home near the cottage had long been overcrowded and no longer in state compliance. KJB made rooms to accommodate 25 little people who may one day be adopted and who have a foster home until that day comes. They will be home-schooled, and in a setting no one will ever hurt them. The barn was a magnificent playhouse and a working farm. Even has a "Bessie, the cow and a 'Kitty Manxy' with a new litter.

Blacki asked, "How did you guys do all of this? KRB said, "Well, Dad, I think you sent me to Law School for a reason. We are not making big changes because nothing fundamentally is broken. I will continue to support Mothers' fight against child abuse in the courts and handle all adoptions and foster care placements in my firm. I also have all state compliances filed and approved so we can move the children from our current small Forever Home and School to the new farm location. It will then enable us to move others who have been on our waiting list too long.

"Father, Mother, KGB spoke up and said, "KAB and I will handle all the day-to-day activities just as we do now, except we will hire a certified school teacher so I can expand our work in Special Education to better serve our young people. KAB will expand his role in the Foundation and fundraising. He has been able to get grants and scholarships to help keep our doors open.

Your little Forever Home and School next to your cottage will be converted into an office. KLB will be the Executive Director of the Board of Directors. KAB will work out of there for all our fundraising efforts. We will all, including you two, of course, be Board members with select community leaders and educators. Those selected will have a sphere of influence to help us grow. KRB will be setting up our non-profit status and taking care of those legalities.

KLB said, "We have tried to follow all the things you and Mother have told us you wanted and the code of ethics for 70 years you have lived by."

Blacki looked at his Andy and said. "When I told you

nearly seventy-five years ago I wanted to be your 'Forever Friend', what I really meant was that I wanted to be your 'Forever Love' and build a 'Forever Home' for our family. Our 5K's, the children whose names all start with the same letter, have made us proud, and leaving them in charge of our legacy is the right thing to do. Andy grinned. "Well, my darling, you certainly exceeded all expectations." "HOWEVER, children, I do not need a title. I AM Andy, the Boss. Blacki said, "Some things never change." The 5K's knew that was coming!

KC jumped up and announced that he was Uncle to 123 children. "None, I mean NONE beat me in Jacks!"

Andy laughed, "I did!"